I0224275

Mangrove

Poems

Bill Hollands

Copyright © 2025 Bill Hollands

All rights reserved. No part of this publication may be reproduced, distributed, or transmitted in any form or by any means, including photocopying, recording, or other electronic or mechanical methods, without the prior written permission of the publisher, except in the case of brief quotations embodied in critical reviews and certain other noncommercial uses permitted by copyright laws. For permission requests, write to the publisher at the address below.

ELJ Editions Ltd. is committed to publishing works of quality and integrity. In that spirit, we are proud to offer this collection to our readers. This is a work of poetry. All views expressed within are Bill Hollands'.

ISBN: 978-1-942004-87-5

Library of Congress Control Number: 2025935874

Cover Art by Andy Sweet and appears in the Letter16 Press book "Shtetl in the Sun: Andy Sweet's South Beach 1977-1980."

ELJ Editions, Ltd.
P.O. Box 815
Washingtonville, NY 10992

www.elj-editions.com

for John and Cooper

Table of Contents

.

I

The Second Ginger Grant

You hit your head and when you wake up
you think you're Ginger. You rehearse lines.
You wear leopard-skin dresses. The other castaways
want you to be Mary Ann again. They don't say
why. They try hypnosis but that makes Gilligan
think *he's* Mary Ann. They come up with a plan—
they'll ask you to put on a show! The professor says
As Ginger she'll want to perform, but underneath
as Mary Ann she'll know she can't. This will create
a tremendous conflict in her mind, and the real world
of Mary Ann will push out the dream world
of Ginger, and Mary Ann will become Mary Ann again.

The show begins. You wear a blue sequined dress,
diamond drop earrings, a white feather boa. You sing
I wanna be loved by you, just you and nobody else
but you. I wanna be loved by you alone, boop-boop-a-doop.
But you're off-key. The castaways cringe, the laugh
track plays, the plan is working! You forget
the words, your eyes full of panic as I take it all in
after school from my living room floor. *Maestro,*
would you start the record again, please? Maybe if I just
dance it I'll be all right. You dance, but it's all wrong.
You trip on the feather boa, fall, and hit your head.
You wake up, you're Mary Ann, what a drag.

Hi. My Name Is Billy Hollands.

And there it is, that little tilt of my head—
We are students from Palmetto Elementary School
and we would like to sing a song for you.
We launch into "Sing, Sing a Song"
as the camera pulls back to reveal
two rows of seated students, hunched over
like birds. Why does everyone look
so sad? Not me, though, see, there I am,
top row center, the only one in a
starched collared shirt, the only one
really selling it. I nod my head, I sway,
I smile with my big teeth. I can smell
the Herbal Essence shampoo on my
shiny hair. Poor kid. The two boys on
either side of me catch each other's eye
and laugh, they're in on the joke, but
what I really remember are the lights,
those bright studio lights, and that little
tilt of the head during my intro, how I
practiced it, where exactly I should
place it, how slight it should be, how
casual, as if I were in motion, as if
I just happened to stop by this
local access TV station on my way
to the future, and even brighter lights,
the Oscars or the Olympics maybe,
and you're so lucky to have caught me
because I can only stay a moment.

Float

I'm Little Jack Horner.
Don't ask why. I wear
knickers, buckled
shoes, a yellow shirt
with a bow. Jack & Jill
and Jack Frost talk
to me. I feign
nonchalance. I poke
my left thumb
in the papier-mâché
plum, wave with my
right. Incandescent
plastic petals flutter—
yellow, orange. I wait
at the end for the queen
and her court. Castle
turrets shake. Crowns
wink. So much
beauty, beauty
beyond understanding.

i want to be clear

nothing   happened
though   he   did
say *you are not
like the others* & how
was   it   we   were
alone with the silent
recorders & triangles
hanging on hooks &
what   did   it   mean
later when he told
the whole class *let's
start with the best* &
why does the film
catch when i see
an old white vw bug?

12 and Under

I *wanted* that yellow ball sitting up high
on the soft green clay for me to drive it
cross-court or down the line, the other kid
flat-footed at the net. And my racquets!
The old wood Jack Kramer Autograph
in its trapezoid press tightened
with wing nuts. The new aluminum Head
in its blue and white nylon cover
I liked to smell. In the shop the teenage boy's
lean tan hands wrapped the grip tight
and strung it with catgut. I balanced it
on my fingertip, bounced a ball on the edge
for fun. The counselor said *Hey Jimmy,*
come look at this as he fed my two-handed
backhand again and again. Back home
alone I slapped the ball against the garage
and aimed for the doorknob. As she watched
through the window did my mother see it
in me before I did? The tentativeness, the
apartness. At tournaments boys swirled
around me as they checked the draw
and then from the crowd *I can't believe*
that faggot is winning until I didn't want
the ball anymore, the racquet a dead thing
in my hand. Oh futility, to skulk to the wall
to hit a few in the true twilight thinking
don't think, don't think, don't think.

Lesson

Terra cotta pots
dot the sills. Velvet
petals cluster over
fleshy leaves, watered
from below. She warns
that a single drop, just
the moisture from my
finger, can turn a leaf
brown. Beyond the cold
glass: mango, lemon,
orange. Palms arc.
Hibiscuses weep.

Presidential Fitness Test

Every year we'd suit up for the ritual
humiliation. Seven demonstrations
of my inadequacy for the red-
faced Phys Ed teacher. Pull-ups
were the worst. I'd eke out one then
fall to the ground and look up
from the dirt at the underside
of his clipboard. Girls did
"hang time" instead, and in 4th grade
Laura Lugar hung in there
for hours. Like a banana
on a hook, she thrust her chin
over the metal bar, curled her body
into a crescent and didn't
budge. We went back to class
and in between decimals and
diagramming sentences the teacher
let us go back outside and have
another look at Laura. In my mind
she's hanging there still in her yellow
uniform against the black dirt
and the pale of the morning sky.

Al's Books and News, Miami

God, I rode there on my bike—
that rust-orange 10-speed, handlebars
like a ram's curled horns. And there's

Al—an ostrich in half-moon glasses,
flannel shirt, and a wool skullcap.
He kept that store cold—a dark

secret around the corner from
the Army Navy and the A&P.
Candy and classics, poetry

next to porn. Al went to the back
to get my *Call of the Wild*
and I slipped a copy of *Blueboy*

into *Life*. My legs shook
and suddenly there's Al, who said,
How about some poetry instead?

Just kidding; that's not what Al said.
But here's the great thing about poetry:
you can change the ending.

Pier at Key West

that boy he's gone
as far as he can go
on the state's bony
finger   archipelago's
end far from parents'
stony waves and out
over the warm salt-
water   that   licks
his belly up through
these weathered slats
is he the watcher or
watched as his cum
surges out before he's
ever   been   touched

A Story

The man's house a mirror of mine. Lose the cat, the potted
plants, flip it once in the air, and I'm home. I was young,

sure, but not *that* young, not sicko young, not call the cops
young. Late teens, mid-to-late teens, mid-teens, call it

sixteen. One day as I gathered my things, he said *Would you like
to go sailing?* I looked at his face, I don't think I had ever

really looked at his face before, his open pleading
eyes, and said *Sure, sailing, sometime, sounds good.* I was nothing

if not polite. What I thought: *Sailing? What is 'sailing'?
I don't understand your language.* I knew English, I knew

sailing. My family owned a small two-person sailboat.
One day my brother Steve and his girlfriend—Patty

was her name—one day they went out in our sailboat
and then pulled it up onto the beach, took a walk, maybe

held hands, got an ice cream in town, who knows?
When they returned, the tide had come in

and the little boat had sailed off without them. But that's
another story, that's another story altogether.

Sex in Portugal

Not sex exactly but in that
ballpark. Not a ballpark! A chapel
of bones. Skulls. Femurs.
Tibias. The—priest?
friar? tour guide?—
before I know it he's got
his arm around my
shoulder and my absurd
hard-on presses up against his
hip, camouflaged somewhat
by his voluminous robe. He's pretty
old, though I guess I wouldn't
think so now. Tourists in their sad
denim shorts (just like mine!)
fondle the bones. The friar
(I'm just going to call him
the friar) points out various
interesting architectural elements
in Portuguese as he pulls me
close and periodically adjusts
our contact. I nod. I don't
understand Portuguese but
it's a beautiful language. Lots
of *zh* sounds. I need to go back
to that chapel. It was cool but
I don't remember much about it.
Story of my life.

No Soap Radio

Tell me anything, I'll believe it. This one time
a man I was going to have sex with told me
that his parrot gave good head. I stared
at that parrot, its stony beak, dark nub
of a tongue, and believed him. Before we
retired to the bedroom, his friends
laughed and laughed. Or the time
another man told me that if I picked up
all the litter around his ice cream truck,
dirty wrappers and such, he'd give me
a free one. My mother stormed
out of the car, so mad that her son
was being taken advantage of like that.
And then there was the story about the kid
who swallowed his tongue. Died right there
on the junior high football field. One day
my brothers and I were playing catch
and the football's pointed tip torpedoed
into my stomach. Knocked the wind
right out of me. I didn't know
what was happening and I ran around
like an idiot with my fingers shoved into
my mouth. Have you ever tried to hold
your tongue? Trust me, it's not easy.

Telling Detail

Wooden desk poet: *Bill Hollands*
sucks dick on weekdays. Or was I still

Billy then? In any case, what struck me
was *on weekdays*—so unexpected

yet true. I've always credited Eddie O'Reilly,
the man's next-door neighbor. Eddie and I

played together sometimes as kids but we had
no chemistry. Simple. Or maybe Eddie

harbored some resentment? Well, the truth is
most high school boys would have seized

on my afterschool activity. I obliterated it,
of course, buried it under black Sharpie—

who would have thought Eddie had it in him
to write a line stuck in my head decades later?

Deciding Game

I slot in ridged thigh plates,
rubber knee pads, squeeze
into girdle pants. My turtle head
emerges from the shell. I'm lost
under helmet, mask. What is
exposed? Twig legs, soft
hands. I'm a fake, a decoy,
my job to run away—
but not today. We've practiced
this play so many times, brutal
practices. On the bus
to the game we sing *We are
the Champions, Another One
Bites the Dust.* But you see
I have a secret. I suck moisture
from the mouth guard molded
to my bite, hear my breath's
echo, underwater snorkeler,
as I swim up the field, turn,
the ball, I know, already
on its way. I could fight off
the defender but I've made
my choice: I let my body
go, just slightly, naked
to the eye. I can, after all,
put on a show. But I drop it,
of course. Adam, Ben,
forgive me, I drop it.

Escape

I sit in the darkened theater and watch
images of naked men on the screen. Is it wrong
to be turned on by a marble sculpture
from the Hellenistic period? Do you know
the story? Laocoön warned the Trojans
about Greeks bearing gifts (see also
Trojan Horse) and the gods sent very big snakes
to punish Laocoön and his sons. The professor
drones on but the message is clear: Sons suffer
for the sins of their father. I, on the other hand,
can't take my eyes off the son on the right.
He looks at his father and his brother and to me
his expression is not *Help* but *I'm out.* Meanwhile
he slyly slips the coiled snake from around
his ankle as if he's shedding a wet
Speedo. I head to the library
and geek out. Apparently, my guy
wasn't even connected to the others
when they unearthed the sculpture's fragments.
Plus, in another version of the story, that son
escapes the snake's jaws altogether. And,
anyway, the whole thing might be a fraud.
One theory goes that it's a forgery by Michelangelo
who passed it off as an antiquity for cash
and you know which son he had *his* eye on.
So on the test when the professor asks
about the paradox of beauty in the midst
of suffering, I write about the liberated son
and take my B and call it good.

I Revisit My Favorite Children's Book, and by Favorite I Mean Most Terrifying

I had a magic pebble, too, but my pebble's magic existed
in my head. And my magic pebble was, in fact, a plastic bead
that I stole from my brother's room and kept like a secret in a little felt box.

One day, or maybe it was many days, or maybe it was many years,
I also *panicked and couldn't think carefully.* I grasped the magic pebble
in my bone-white hand and wished I were a rock. And so it came to be.

My parents did not wander the village in search of me.
My parents did not look at each other with *great sorrow.*
My parents did not have a picnic on me and eat *timothy compote.*

I, too, wanted to shout *Mother! Father! I'm right here!* But I didn't
look like a rock, I looked like a boy. And I was not *stone-dumb.*
Words such as *yes* and *no* crept out of my mouth.

Night came with many stars. Seasons occurred. *Strawberry Hill*
grew cold, then hot, then cold again. Wolves howled on me.
And if the story ends there, what then?

II

Chuckles Bites the Dust

The beloved clown is dead—
grand marshal of the circus parade,
dressed as Peter Peanut, crushed
by an elephant. The gang is sad
for a while. Ted's a bit shell-shocked
since *he* was supposed to be
grand marshal, but Mr. Grant
wouldn't let him and now Ted
understands the arbitrariness
of death. Then Murray starts up
with the jokes: *It could have been worse—*
you know how hard it is to stop
after just one peanut, etc. Mr. Grant
giggles, Sue Ann joins in, and it's up
to Mary in her trim pantsuit
to scold them. A man has died
after all. The gang is chastened. Mary
plans a televised tribute featuring
Chuckles' most beloved characters—
Peter Peanut, of course, but also
Billy Banana, Mr. Fee-Fi-Fo-Fum,
Aunt Yoo-Hoo. The tribute will close
with Chuckles' famous clown credo—
A little song, a little dance, a little seltzer
down your pants. Later, at the funeral
(Georgette's there too) Murray floats
one more joke, Mary says *enough*
is enough, and Murray promises *no more*
jokes. Everyone is solemn. The reverend
begins to speak (something about
Chuckles and his archrival
Señor Kaboom) and Mary

starts to laugh. Just a small whimper
at first, then she clears her throat, then
it's almost a moan, she's trying
so hard to hold it in. The reverend says
*There was always some deeper meaning
to whatever Chuckles did* and that's
when Mary loses it, she can't
contain it any longer, she's alone
in her laughter and her pain
and she can't stop, she simply
cannot stop.

In Which I Search Zillow® for My Childhood Home and Discover It's for Sale

Our modest 1950's rambler
now *mid-century modern*, façade
crisp white. 40 years, 3000
miles, one click and I'm

in. *Everything* is white—
the walls, the fireplace, even
the living room's old wood
paneling. No more murky

fish tank. Faux fir floors glisten,
wall-to-wall all gone. I grew up
here? *3D Walkthrough* arrows
show me the way. I stumble

forward, pull up short, lurch
again, a drunk, a toddler,
a robot on the fritz. I zip
down the hallway (wasn't it

longer?) to my brother's room,
then my room—no more
shelves for my beer can
collection. Walls slant

crazily as I careen around
corners. Why can't I
find my parents' room? How
do I back up? I stagger

to the kitchen, a movie
set of stainless steel
and granite. Through it all
the staged furniture

poses, Scandinavian blond
wood, no clutter of records,
trophies, dog bowls, *Sports
Illustrated*. I need

air, so I click *Street View*
and pan around the old
neighborhood, now
gated McMansions.

*Charming family home.
Move-in ready. Enjoy as is
or tear down and build
the home of your dreams!*

Old Cutler Road

A cut across the grid. Let's begin
again where the Everglades
end and follow history's
limestone ridge. Banyans vault
to the ribs. Look. My family
drags a net off Matheson Hammock.
My brother has a parrot on his head.
I am in the trees.

Cleo in Florida

Satellite image a blurry swirl around
a dark eye like a fetal ultrasound, I
seven months in your belly, you
unpacking boxes. What was this place?

Thirty-nine, three boys plus three
miscarriages, whatever happened
I'd be the last. You'd heard the old
wives' tale, storms and labor, so

you steadied your breath as you
searched for flashlights and tracked
the path directly to you. Neighbors
(strangers) offered mistaken advice:

Tape an X on every window. Run
the sprinklers to empty the pool.
Run the sprinklers? The boys
slept right through it, but you

listened all night. What was that
sound? Endless freight train? Woman
screaming? Fruit and palm fronds
pounded the house, but I

stayed in. Bleary-eyed you picked
your way over the toppled
ficus tree, roots where branches
should be. Muse of history,

your son learned the lyre
from his lovers, that's true,
but his eye is always on you,
always on a path to you.

Youngest Child

Spoiled, sure, but also
alone—pushing that little
toy car across cool
speckled linoleum, or
pelting a tennis ball against
the back wall as silver
evening envelops. First
to bed he counts to three
hundred then slips
through the empty
dark rooms. A folded
dish towel drapes over
the counter. Such familiar
sounds from the living
room—television,
laughter—my family,
how did I know?

The Bird Feeder

It hangs there on a string, a house with windows,
brown and still. *Something to look at*—your words,

though they're true for me today. A dead rose
in a door—this attracts the hummingbirds.

White dots of light scatter in the woods. All day
you look out, reel off names as you squint your eyes:

sparrow, cardinal, sparrow, blue jay.
Mom and I nod, say *yes*, hover close by.

Last night, like a chill: *Find someone soon,*
you said. *You'll wonder where your chances went.*

We were reading, we were in the living room;
I thought even, even this: *We are content*—

Too many birds now. A cry, and wings unfurl.
The perch tilts, the opening for food inches

to a close. This is meant to ward off squirrels.
Finches. I can hear you say it. *Male finches.*

Parrot Jungle Polaroid, Miami, April 1981

That's Mom's handwriting on the back.
You've got a parrot on your head
and two more on your outstretched
arms—one of them seems to be going
for your ear lobe. Your new fiancée
has her three parrots, too. Your pale
winter legs will no doubt turn pink
by the end of this day. You both
smile for the camera in that *can-you-believe-*
we-have-parrots-on-our-heads way. And why
not? You're at the beginning, or
if not the beginning exactly, at least
the beginning of something. You can't
yet know that yours will be a half-
life, no one thinks like that, and besides,
those parrots on your heads must hurt,
what with your hair just starting to thin
and your wife (soon-to-be wife/widow)
with her buzz cut that we all found
so interesting. Did the tour guide
tell you that some parrots live
to be over one hundred years old? Well,
it's rare, but it does happen, especially
with macaws, and those babies
are definitely macaws.

Thief

Black wing-
tips, yours, mine
now. Two crows
curled, concealing
tongues. Waxy
laces worm
through eyelets. I
lift them from
their nest. My
gold toes offer
brief life.

The Age of Innocence

It's on TV in the hotel room
        after. Three brothers (three
  now) in our dark
            disheveled suits. The late sun
      is everywhere in the room.

I remember we played together. Being here makes me remember so much.

I look at my brothers. Their smiles
          tell me they see it, too, the life
    Michelle Pfeiffer brings to this scene,
              even Daniel Day-Lewis laughs,
      how could he not?

You have been away a very long time.
        Oh, centuries and centuries.

Already a bit day-drunk we crack open
          the mini-bar's little bottles and bags,
  who cares? I remember
          we watched those miniseries together—
    Roots, Rich Man Poor Man...

Since you're not tired and want to talk there's something I have to tell you.
    Oh yes, dear. Something about yourself?

Home from your junior year abroad
         we were somehow alone that week we watched
    Brideshead Revisited. Long hair, bearded,
         you rolled your own cigarettes, I worried
      it was marijuana, what did I know?

I'm tired of everything. I want to get away, go somewhere far.
             How far?
     I don't know. I thought of India. Or Japan.
                   As far as that?

When did it get dark? We don't want the movie to end
             but it does, of course. We leave everything
     a mess—empty bottles and bags, crumpled
                   suits on the floor, three brothers split
             between two queen beds.

Sunburn

Center piece, middle
Brother, you left an
Incomplete poem

Or should I say my
Memory is partial,
The heart of it gone

> *Invisible ink*
> *(   )*
> *Turning it to red*

Miami Youth Fair
Blue ribbon winner,
High school haiku, just

Seven syllables—
Reader, I tried, I
Cannot finish it

Notes on My Mother's Desk

Command central in the kitchen with
       the empty space
          underneath where I liked to hide. A calendar tacked to corkboard
               tracked the lives of your four boys—

tee-ball practice, cub scout banquet, orthodontist. A worn journal
       hidden/not hidden
          in the drawer documented chicken poxes, mumps vaccinations,
             my brown recluse spider bite, your three

"missed abortions"—how I stared at
       those words.
     A Rolodex tallied Christmas cards: year, S for sent, R for received.
        A metal letter opener you told me never

to stick in the light socket. (After that I could never not think about
       the light socket.)
     And the pocket spiral notepads where you planned our 6:00 dinners:
          meat loaf, creamed tuna fish on toast, hash. Later

when my brothers made their Sunday night long-distance calls
       I watched you
         sit at that desk, the phone's cord twisting into knots as you took notes
            on those little notepads, curled leaves of memory:

Chip – job good – marathon next weekend
Pete – job good – Red Sox game – Springsteen concert
Steve –

puzzle

always in progress
in my mind
never done mother
at the rickety card
table vast field
of flowers or snow-
capped peaks tabs
blanks the end-
less blue sky

Revision

In college I wrote a poem about my mother.
This isn't surprising. Not
a kind poem—in particular,
the last word. Such a good word,
the professor said. Please don't ask me
to repeat it here. The other students
expressed great sympathy for
the poem's speaker, a young man
strikingly similar to myself. The poem
was accepted for publication
by the college magazine, of which
I was the editor, and I presented it
to my mother for Christmas,
a proud son indeed. Perhaps nothing

about this story is surprising, including
the fact that when the time came
I found the old magazine
at the bottom of a box in the back
of a dark closet. What good
is poetry? Robert Hass says
to put the problem in the poem.
Here's the problem: I loved my mother.
I loved my mother, and she is dead.
I loved my mother, she is dead,
and I never told her I was sorry.
There you have it. Yes, of course,

I've revised the poem.
You wouldn't even recognize it now.
Some people say that when a poet
searches for a poem's heart

and cuts a stanza here, a line there,
even just one word, a shadow remains,
shadow of what's no longer there.

Dragging for Fish

Knee-deep in the warm brackish
water off Matheson Hammock
we stretch the net between us
and collect whatever comes
our way. Your wet hand
combs the brown seaweed
to uncover silver needlefish
and guppies, puffers swelling
in the dry heat. A yellow seahorse
if we're lucky. Mangroves
watch. The brain shrinks
and what remains is feeling.
In the end you didn't know me,
you just knew I was someone important.

Church Steps

                    then I heard it

    my name   turned and

            he opened his arms

Bill   and my father

            he opened his arms

like an offer   to dance

        October   already so

                cold   oh how

puzzling it was

                    to watch him dance

My Father on Stage, Briefly Alone

Community theater, *The Gin Game*—
you're old but not *that* old. Vigorous,

as Pete likes to say. You and your "wife"
take the stage, cards are dealt, the game

begins. Suddenly she stands, says she forgot
her glasses, exits the stage, leaves you

alone. Does the audience know
this isn't in the script? In the dark

I'm certain this shouldn't happen, why
is this happening? A shade

flits across your face, a blank sheet
in wind. But you keep your cool, invent

a funny bit where you peek at her cards, swap
one of hers for one of your own, perfectly

in character. The audience laughs. Your wife
who is not your wife returns. The play resumes.

Portrait of My Father with the Letter V

Valedictorian. Ivy League. A virgin
when you married, or so you said
when we had "the talk." To me you were all
Aqua Velva and a vodka martini in the evening,
two olives on a toothpick. You taught me
to replace a divot and how to pronounce
vichyssoise. Avowed Democrat. Achievement
a must. In your prime unbeatable
in Trivial Pursuit and a suave dancer
to boot. Vain enough to own a toupee
but kept it hidden. Private? Veiled?
Reserved, for sure. Did you grieve
for your son and wife? Poetry lover,
you'd have preferred something formal here—
a villanelle perhaps, and you'd have known
what that meant. Dad, I'm sorry
this is simple free verse. Nevertheless,
a valediction. You were all vim
and vigor to the very end. Covid death
number twenty-five thousand, give
or take, now vapor.

I Search My Father's Playbill Collection but Don't Find What I'm Looking For, Whatever That Is

Ten black binders, neatly chronological. First: *The Glass Menagerie*, Broadway,
    1946. Just sixteen, a senior (skipped a grade, smart boy). Special

trip with your parents? Only child, as you sat in the dark did you see yourself
    as Tom, aspiring poet who dreams of escape? Or fear

you'd be the gentleman caller, former popular high school athlete
    now a shipping clerk at a shoe warehouse? Next, college, the city

and classic productions: *The Country Girl, Mr. Roberts, Born Yesterday*.
    Musicals, too: *South Pacific, The King and I, Kiss Me Kate*. Post-war,

heady times, drinks at the Algonquin. Brando, Burton, Cobb,
    Gielgud, Harrison, Fonda. Is this why you kept them, for us to marvel

at the stars? Then, domesticity—less Broadway, more touring companies
    wherever we lived: *Mame* in Miami, *Amadeus* in D.C. So much

Sondheim. Retirement, and at last you take to the stage! Community theater
    lead roles right off the bat: *The Gin Game, The Cocktail Hour,*

On Golden Pond. Not the best actor, Pete says, too self-conscious
    but I disagree: like all great stars, at once both your character

and yourself, impossible to separate. But where are you? I look
    in the binders for the programs from this last explosion of light

but you didn't save them. All I find are second-tier stars in regional revivals:
    A Delicate Balance, Death of a Salesman, A Streetcar Named Desire.

Stiltsville, Biscayne Bay

Lonely sentinels watch
                fishermen thread
     finger channels
               between them. Salt-
water licks cracked
         wood pilings. Night
and the light-
       house beam rakes
             hollowed faces.

Spoons

It hardly seems possible
that I could be so
focused on my own
cards—the grabbing
from the left, passing
to the right—that I would
miss my brother entirely
as he reaches his hand
to the table's center, takes
one spoon, and then
years later my mother
and my father in silence
collect their spoons until
I am left still searching
for my four of a kind when
I finally look up, the table
has been cleared, and everyone
is holding up a spoon.

III

The Love Boat

You've jetted in from Fantasy Island and you're thinking,
Puerto Vallarta again? Julie directs you to your cabin
on the Aloha deck, then does a quick line
on her clipboard. You wonder whether this time
your storyline will be comedy, romantic comedy, or drama.
You wander the corridors where the other passengers
are already fucking behind their cabin doors when you run
into Captain Stubing, who quit his job as a news writer
to follow this dream. You get to your cabin
and are surprised to find David Cassidy standing there
in a towel. You say there must be some mistake
and he says Hi roomie! so you decide to just
go with it. You become best friends. The ship's horn
blows and you follow Charo as she cuchi cuchi's up
to the deck. Confetti explodes. Goodbye, Jo Anne Worley!
Goodbye, Barbi Benton and Adrienne Barbeau!
Suzanne Somers and Elke Sommer sulk on shore
but what can you do? There's only so much room
on this ship. You and David down some shots then decide
to grab a bite. At the next table Scott Baio is trying to flirt
with Kristy McNichol by doing The Claw. He's such
a goof! Scott, you're barking up the wrong tree!
Meredith Baxter can't decide whether to keep the Birney,
date Bill Bixby, or become a lesbian. Meanwhile,
you can't deny it, you're developing feelings
for David. He sheepishly agrees to take the stage
and perform *I Think I Love You*, but why is he singing
to Florence Henderson and not to you? First of all,
David, she's too old for you. Second of all…wait,
is that Eva and Zsa Zsa Gabor behind the bar
having a three-way with the ship's doctor? You feel
dizzy. Luckily, Dr. Joyce Brothers is on hand
to offer you learned and practical advice, as always.

The Crocodile Pit, Miami Serpentarium

There is, of course, the story
about Clarabelle, that big one
they were all so proud of.
The boy's mother sat him up
on the ledge, then he toppled in,
and the owner came out with a rifle
and shot Clarabelle that very night.
I circle to find the biggest one
left. Through a hole in the dense mesh
of gray branches a series of bumps,
fifteen feet long at least, ripples
the pond's surface, dead center.
When no one is watching I drop
my chocolate bar in the pit. It hesitates
just for a moment, then the long tail
sways back and forth in the water until
splayed toes glide the heavy body up,
quick, onto the grass and through the mesh,
crossing over to me where it stabs
the chocolate bar in its snout, awkwardly,
and jiggles it down. Delighted screams
of school children come through me
from the King Cobra Show going on
inside. And it gazes up at me, wanting
more, I suppose, as if I might think
they didn't feed very well here.
Its scaly skin is like a coat of barnacles
stuck to an old log. A layer of shingled tiles
runs along its back. It smells of musk
and it's green all over, dark olive green
and thick, like if you sliced right through
its hide and into its middle, it would all be,

all of it, green and hard. I stare it down
until it turns around and drags its fat body
along the ground, the way you think
it should move all the time. It settles
back down into the pond. Someone
brushes my shoulder, says, *Let's go, babe,*
and all I can see when I twirl around
are my lover's three moles through a thin,
dark beard, his hard little eyes, all that green.

there's a coldness in me

a coldness i say deep deep
deep beneath the beating
heart i imagine it a block
of ice tiny boy doll frozen
a figurine many are they
have tried to free him me
included warm breath i
thank you such a wee thing

Examination

I am laid out, strange
chicken under heat lamp
as she feathers my head
to expose blue scalp, stretches
the wax webbing between
my toes. Who else
looks at me this closely?
Bug-eyed, inscrutable,
she ponders the great mystery
of my back, inks what must be
frozen or gouged out—
barnacles, dirty warts, moles
in hiding. Fecund eco-
system of death and desire,
what good my thousand lovers?

Return

Halfway through I found myself
in woods. I mean actual
swamp. I was a child here
after all, unearthing
rusted cans as men perched
in trees. Did I mention
the trees? Ancient banyans, mesh
of mangrove root reaching down
under water. Where water ends
and land begins is hard
to say. I lay in muck. What was it
you said? *You don't remember
do you*—something
along these lines. It was the tone
that reached me, call of one
seaside sparrow. I got up. Mud
spread thick across my face.

Courtship

I gave you crabs and you let us
pretend that it might have been
you who gave them to me and that
was so lovely. On our first
proper date you wore penny loafers
and never wore them again and I
never thanked you for that. Second date
and I cried at dinner, just sobbed
and sobbed until my tears
became a stream with little fish
in it. On Fire Island that summer
we rented a small sailboat though
neither of us really knew how to sail
and as the ferry barreled down on us
I'm so glad we got the big fight
out of our system. And that night
as your friends and I played Trivial
Pursuit or Pictionary, you sat
by yourself on the couch and read
How We Die and that, my love, that
is when I knew for sure. Let's
not even talk about the cat.

Mr. Hollands Explains His Tattoo to His Students

Early October. I know it's coming.

We're discussing To Kill a Mockingbird
and a hand shoots up in the back.

Mr. Hollands, what does your tattoo mean?

The other students, previously semi-
comatose, perk up, grateful
for their classmate's audacity.

They wait.

I know what it means,
their question. It means
Oh Mr. Hollands we like you
sort of, maybe, not completely
sure yet, please
be a little real with us, please
tell us something real.

Three black bars on my right forearm,
an early late middle age addition.
I don't know what it means.

They wait.

So I lie to them. I say
This is my family.
One bar for my husband,
one for our son
and one for me.
Three individuals
making a whole.

They seem semi-satisfied.
One girl says *Aw.*

We return to the book.
Atticus tells his children *It's a sin
to kill a mockingbird* and I explain
that the mockingbird
represents innocence

when probably it was just
something Harper Lee's father said
and she remembered it because
she loved her father, perhaps
feared him a little bit, too.

My students write
mockingbird = innocence.

And I stand in front of the class.
Like an idiot magician
I place my hand over the tattoo
and watch it disappear.
When I take my hand away
it reappears.

Next up: Macbeth.

Spin the Globe

Close your eyes as the ridges
tick by under your fingertip.
Wherever you land you go,
do-overs allowed, as many
as you like. Madagascar, Nepal,
Suriname, Chad—I always
wanted Chad. I knew
nothing about it.

My son and I take a road trip
each summer, just us, special
time. In the hotel room I
spread out my old road atlas,
try to show him the big
picture. *See, first Bend, then
Crater Lake, then Ashland.* He
rolls his eyes, so I let it go

and read about Chad. Wikipedia
says it's a mess—poverty,
corruption, violence. We're advised
not to go there, and if you're gay
forget it. But there must be
beauty, of course, joy even, small
moments maybe, and I still
know next to nothing about it.

Old Flame

Look at it one way, all of it
makes sense, like a young

child who plants one
foot in front of the other, walking

or falling, it's hard to say,
but there's a logic

to each step, and a goal,
you can't say there's not, maybe

that lightbulb on the table
(what's it doing there

anyway?) but he never
gets there, he gets

sidetracked and besides
that's not how you're looking at it,

is it, not now, not
tonight, when it's so easy

to hit send, as if thirty-five years
were nothing, a momentary

darkness erased with the twist
of a bulb, as if the light

and the heat were there
all along, which they are.

Near Miss

Live long enough and you'll have a few
if you're lucky. Take me, for instance—
when my son crossed the street
and the car's tires screamed and his body
arced into a *C*. Or once in the doctor's
cold office when the air froze into a word.

Or maybe it's a choice—your choice,
the other person's, doesn't matter. You sit
on the edge of the bed in the hotel room,
run your hand over the quilted bedspread
and wait for the answer. It's not much really,
not much that determines a life.

The Painting

I asked my husband for art
this Christmas. No sweater, no
kitchen gadget. *But I want
something by Rob. It's good
to support our artist friends, yes?*

Little impressionist landscapes
painted on wooden blocks.
Up close just brushstrokes
but back up and everything
becomes clear. *You choose.*

You know what came next.
He picked this dark thing?
I wanted rich browns, deep
greens, a dash of yellow or red—
autumnal, sure, but *alive.*

Instead, black trees,
a gray sky, one gash
of white. There's even a crack
in the block. Was that there
from the beginning?

The cold months pass
and I remember the painting.
Who knows why? I lift it down
from the high shelf, surprised
by its heft in my hand. And look,

a stamp on the back: *4x4 Satsop No. 45.*
What could that mean? I cradle it

in my palm, turn it this way
and that as it catches the light
and I decide to love it.

Proposal

Pauline Kael wrote that Divine's performance
in *Hairspray* has a "what-the-hell quality"
the film needs. I feel the same way
about our marriage, don't you? Here's
our joke: When I said at the restaurant
I was "ready to take the next step"
you thought I meant marriage
when what I really meant was dessert.
(Our son likes to tell that one.)
Is it true? Does it matter?
I can't remember that far back
and we were probably drunk anyway.
But you know what they say—
in every joke there's a grain of truth.

What *did* I mean? Nobody talked about
marriage in those days. Commitment,
I suppose—a willingness to stick with it.
But whatever it was I offered
you accepted, one link in a long
necklace of what-the-hells, Divine
as Edna Turnblad in her sleeveless
cotton dress, ironing and tutting and
calling out to her child, shaking
her head and ironing some more.

On My Morning Walk It Occurs to Me that My Name is Similar to Billy Collins

A man is doing lunges in the park
but I don't even notice him until
I take a picture of the remarkable
sunrise and send it to the family
group chat (no response, still
asleep?) and there he is in the lower
right corner. I suppose he wants to make
efficient use of time, stuck as he is
flinging the dog ball over and over
and over again. And then it dawns
on me. How have I never thought of it
before? After all, I was Billy until
what, college? Despite the humiliating
songs, my burning fourth-grade face—
Can you bake a cherry pie, Billy Boy,
Billy Boy? Billy, don't be a hero, don't be a
fool with your life. And now here
is the part of the poem where you say
OK, *Billy,* but what about the last name?
Hear me out: Whenever I try to say it
and my throat closes as it always does
and the thin sound threads its way out,
people look at me, puzzled, and say
Collins? The man in the park
is still doing lunges as I head home,
take down a few books and study
the dust jackets. Not a bad looking guy
when he was younger, kind of sexy even
if you're into imps. I read. You know,
I never gave my mother a lanyard

like Billy did, my mother who named me,
though I did make her an ashtray once, blue
misshapen thing. It sat on her desk
for years collecting ashes from
the cigarettes that would have killed her
if the Alzheimer's hadn't gotten to her
first. Well. I see now that it's time
for my own dog's walk. He glances
over at me just once, his second-string
demigod, as he leads my husband
right out the front door.

A Rare Sighting

My son spent the better part of today
following people on TikTok whose usernames
recreate the lyrics of Rick Astley's 1987 hit
"Never Gonna Give You Up." There is,
of course, so much to say about this—
the jolt of satisfaction he must feel when,
for example, he finds someone whose name is
and or *to*. It is, perhaps, not so very different
from what I feel now writing these lines. But here
is the part that's not in the parenting books, how
when he walks into the kitchen to show you
how many he's found so far, and you're trying
to make dinner but the dog is barking because
there's an Amazon guy on the porch
you don't ask why, you don't say *Good lord*
go read a book. Instead you tell yourself
Plant your feet, stay as he towers over you now
from behind and holds his phone over
your shoulder to show you, and then
leans his head against your head, relaxes
his body against your body, until it becomes
a joke, of course, you're making each other
fall now, and finally you have to say *OK stop*
I need to make this spaghetti. But for those
few moments it was as if an animal
had wandered out of the woods and into
your kitchen, a moose perhaps, partially
domesticated, a moose in a hoodie, and placed
his snout over the fence of your shoulder,
his breath warm, fur soft, smell moosey,
before ambling away to find his kind.

Walk of Shame

Not that kind. I mean I literally
walk each morning and think about
my shame—shame of the body,
the mind, shame of my
shame. Will it end? Yesterday
all was clear yet I heard
the sky crack then
a huge cedar branch whooshed
to the ground. There was no
reason for it, none
that I could see. Today
the torn limb's jagged, still
fresh, the trunk's wound
shrouded by a thousand leaves.

Dogs

Those were the days that dogs ran wild.
Shit everywhere. Not unusual to meet
their end from a speeding car. My parents
made me take one last look at Twinkie
laid out on a blood-flecked towel
in the back of the family station wagon.
Then we got Spooky. I'm not saying
we weren't sad, I just don't remember
dwelling on it. Still, it was something
to see, old Twinkie struggling for a few
final breaths. Last night my son
got into a wreck. Not a tragedy, nobody
hurt. Rain, curve in the road, teenager,
what can you do? But the more we
looked at it, the worse it got. No tire
should come to rest at that angle,
for example. When we confirmed
it was a total loss, he said *I made
a mistake* and the blood rushed away
from his face. There are places
the imagination should not go. Today
I returned. I wanted to see it in daylight,
maybe clear up any debris. I ran my hand
over the cold light pole, stared down
at bits from the shattered headlight
as they blinked across a gash of mud.

I Stayed Quiet

Prove to me you're conscious,
my son says, *in the same way*
I'm conscious. I look up
from the half-mashed
potatoes—his eyes
are wild. Must these
epiphanies always occur
in the kitchen? Outside
shouts of neighbor kids
fade. I sit on a stool
as my mother tosses
that night's salad,
hands me crisp
lettuce leaves dipped
in green goddess
dressing. Amber
light. Summer? At least
the sun remains.

Tree

I'm fifty-nine and just starting
to see them. Before
when I put one in a poem
it was only for a bit of local color—
a palm tree here, a mangrove there—
the trees of my childhood
mostly. Or maybe I needed
a metaphor—roots and all that.

There's one I like in Volunteer Park,
a slippery elm. I looked up
what it was on my app.
It doesn't belong here, of course,
what does? Olmsted probably
told someone to plant it here
a long time ago. At some point
we must leave our origin story behind.

I cannot tell you my need
to see it every day. Some days
I notice the great branches, others
the tender leaves. You will say
I'm still just seeing myself,
that the tree's existence proves to me
my own. No doubt
you are right, but still.

Notes

Though I wrote "The Second Ginger Grant" before I had read Tim Dlugos' "Gilligan's Island" or David Trinidad's "Essay with Movable Parts" (which is also, in part, about that television series), I do want to tip my hat to these two great poets and poems.

"No Soap Radio" is a practical joke in which one person in a group doesn't know that the punchline is meaningless.

"I Revisit My Favorite Children's Book, and by Favorite I Mean Most Terrifying" refers to, and borrows lines from, William Steig's classic children's book *Sylvester and the Magic Pebble*, first published and copyright Simon and Schuster, 1969.

"Chuckles Bites the Dust" refers to the famous episode by that name from the 1970's television series *The Mary Tyler Moore Show*.

Martin Scorsese's screen adaptation of Edith Wharton's novel *The Age of Innocence* was released in 1993.

Stiltsville is a group of now-abandoned wooden stilt houses built one mile off the coast of Cape Florida.

The Love Boat television series aired from 1977 to 1986.

"On My Morning Walk It Occurs to Me that My Name is Similar to Billy Collins" makes reference to Billy Collins' great poem "The Lanyard."

Acknowledgements

Many thanks to the editors of the following journals in which these poems first appeared:

The Account: "In Which I Search Zillow® for My Childhood Home and Discover It's for Sale"

The Adroit Journal: "Portrait of My Father with the Letter V"

The American Journal of Poetry: "Chuckles Bites the Dust" (under the title "Confessional Poem")

Autofocus: "My Father, on Stage, Briefly Alone"

Birmingham Poetry Review: "Spoons"

Boulevard: "I Revisit My Favorite Children's Book, and by Favorite I Mean Most Terrifying"

& Change: "Pier at Key West"

CIRQUE: "The Age of Innocence"

Columba: "Old Cutler Road"

DIAGRAM: "The Crocodile Pit, Miami Serpentarium" and "Deciding Game"

The Ekphrastic Review: "Escape"

The Florida Review: "Walk of Shame"

Figure 1: "No Soap Radio"

Gigantic Sequins: "Dragging for Fish"

The Greensboro Review: "Al's Books and News, Miami"

Hawai`i Pacific Review: "Spin the Globe"

Hole in the Head Review: "Examination"

Hunger Mountain Review: "Tree"

The Indianapolis Review: "Cleo in Florida"

The Inflectionist Review: "puzzle" and "there's a coldness in me"

Jelly Bucket: "Telling Detail"

Litbreak Magazine: "Courtship," "Proposal," "Mr. Hollands Explains His Tattoo to His Students," and "On My Morning Walk It Occurs to Me that My Name is Similar to Billy Collins"

Narrative Northeast: "Sunburn"

New Ohio Review: "Near Miss"

No Contact: "Sex in Portugal"

North American Review: "A Story" and "Youngest Child"

One: "A Rare Sighting"

PageBoy Magazine: "The Bird Feeder"

Pine Hills Review: "The Second Ginger Grant" (under the title "Another Ginger Grant")

Plume: "Hi. My Name is Billy Hollands."

Poetry Northwest: "I Stayed Quiet" and "i want to be clear"

Pontoon Poetry: "The Painting"

Rattle: "Presidential Fitness Test"

Rappahannock Review: "Notes on My Mother's Desk"

Raleigh Review: "Church Steps"

Sepia: "The Love Boat"

The Shore: "Dogs"

Smartish Pace: "Old Flame"

The Summerset Review: "12 and Under"

3Elements Literary Review: "Parrot Jungle Polaroid, Miami, April 1981"

Tipton Poetry Journal: "Thief"

Watershed Review: "Float"

Whale Road Review: "I Search My Father's Playbill Collection but Don't Find What I'm Looking For, Whatever That Is"

wildness: "Lesson," "Return" and "Stiltsville, Biscayne Bay"

The Worcester Review: "Revision"

"Portrait of My Father with the Letter V" was republished on *The Slowdown* podcast.

"Courtship" and "Proposal" were republished in *The Gay & Lesbian Review*.

"Chuckles Bites the Dust" (aka "Confessional Poem") was republished in *Bulb Culture Collective*.

"The Bird Feeder" and "Thief" were republished in *Abstract Magazine*.

"The Love Boat" and "A Rare Sighting" were republished in *Pontoon Poetry*.

"Hi. My Name Is Billy Hollands." and "A Rare Sighting" were republished in the *Queer Poetry Anthology*, a project of the Washington State Poet Laureate.

My deepest gratitude to:

Ariana Den Bleyker and Keith J. Powell at ELJ Editions for your tireless work on behalf of your authors.

Ellen Bass, Denise Duhamel, and David Trinidad for your kind and generous words in support of this book.

Andy Sweet (rest in peace) for your beautiful cover photograph, and Edward Christin and the Sweet family for preserving Andy's legacy.

My teachers Lawrence Raab, Lisa Haines Wright, Katha Pollitt, Keetje Kuipers, Bill Carty, and especially Louise Glück (rest in peace) and Jeanine Walker, both of whom, at different points in my life, changed my life.

My fellow poets River Elizabeth Hall, Chase Ferree, Kimberly Kralowec,

Cindy Buchanan, Seth Rosenbloom, Brooke Lehmann, Judy Aks, Paula Sternberg, Patricia Joslin, and Todd Campbell for your camaraderie and invaluable feedback on this manuscript and the poems therein.

Kathleen Alcalá, the 2025 Jack Straw cohort, and everyone at the Jack Straw Cultural Center for your fellowship and support.

All my friends from Miami, Williams, New York, Seattle, Palm Springs, and beyond, too many to name: I love and appreciate you all.

My husband and son, to whom this book and so much else is dedicated.

My brothers, sisters-in-law, nieces, and nephews, for your love, support, and annual reunions. And in memory of my parents and my brother Steve; this is also for you.

About the Author

Bill Hollands grew up in Miami, Florida and graduated from Williams College and Cambridge University. His poems have appeared in such journals as *The Adroit Journal*, *New Ohio Review*, *The Southern Review*, *Poetry Northwest*, *Smartish Pace*, *Birmingham Poetry Review*, *The Greensboro Review*, *Rattle*, *DIAGRAM*, *North American Review*, and *Plume*, as well as on *The Slowdown* podcast. A multiple Best of the Net and Pushcart nominee, he is a 2025 Jack Straw Writing Fellow. He lives in Seattle with his husband and their son.

Photo by Adrianne Mathiowetz.

www.ingramcontent.com/pod-product-compliance
Lightning Source LLC
Chambersburg PA
CBHW020213090426
42734CB00008B/1056

* 9 7 8 1 9 4 2 0 0 4 8 7 5 *